from Anabaptist Seed

from Anabaptist Seed

Exploring the historical center of Anabaptist teachings and practices

C. Arnold Snyder

Commissioned by Mennonite World Conference

Co-published with Pandora Press

Good Books

Intercourse, PA 17534
800/762-7171
www.GoodBooks.com

From Anabaptist Seed is published in cooperation with Mennonite World Conference (MWC) and has been selected for its Global Anabaptist-Mennonite Shelf of Literature. MWC chooses one book each year and urges its member churches to translate and study the book, in an effort to develop a common body of literature. **From Anabaptist Seed** is now available in 15 languages: English, French, Spanish, Portuguese, Dutch, German, Japanese, Chinese, Korean, Indonesian, Hindi, Telugu, Amharic, and Vietnamese.

Mennonite World Conference is a global community of Christian churches who trace their beginning to the 16th-century Radical Reformation in Europe, particularly to the Anabaptist movement. Today, close to 1,300,000 believers belong to this faith family; at least 60 percent are African, Asian, or Latin American.

MWC represents 95 Mennonite and Brethren in Christ national churches from 51 countries on six continents.

Mennonite World Conference exists to (1) be a global community of faith in the Anabaptist tradition, (2) facilitate community among Anabaptist-related churches worldwide, and (3) relate to other Christian world communions and organizations.

MWC's headquarters are in Strasbourg, France. For more information, visit its website at www.mwc-cmm.org.

Cover photograph by Howard Zehr

Design by Cliff Snyder
FROM ANABAPTIST SEED

International Standard Book Number: 978-1-56148-585-7
Library of Congress Catalog Card Number: 2007040514

Originally published by Pandora Press (Kitchener, ON) and Herald Press (Scottdate, PA), ©1999

Library of Congress Cataloging-in-Publication Data

Snyder, C. Arnold, 1946-
From Anabaptist seed / by C. Arnold Snyder.
p. cm.
Originally published: Kitchener, Ont. : Pandora Press ; Scottdale, Pa. : Herald Press, c1999.
ISBN 978-1-56148-585-7 (alk. paper)
1. Anabaptists--Doctrines. I. Title.
BX4931.3.S69 2007
284'.3--dc22 2007040514

Table of Contents

Preface 3

Introduction 5

1. Anabaptist Doctrines **8**

How can we know God's will? 9

For Discussion 12

How are we saved? 12

For Discussion 16

Consequences of Anabaptist Doctrines 17

For Discussion 19

2. Anabaptist Church Ordinances **20**

Baptism 22

For Discussion 25

Church Discipline 26

For Discussion 28

The Lord's Supper 28
For Discussion 30
Footwashing 31
For Discussion 32
Consequences of Anabaptist Ordinances 32
For Discussion 34
3. Discipleship: Living the Faith **35**
Truth-telling 36
For Discussion 37
Economic Sharing 38
For Discussion 39
Pacifism 40
For Discussion 45
4. Conclusion **46**
For Discussion 51
About the Author 52

Preface

Today over one million Christians are members of churches which sprouted more or less directly "from Anabaptist seed." Who are these Christians? What do they believe? How do they act? What in fact do they hold in common? "Good questions," many of us who belong to this confessional family might say. "But we are not entirely sure of the answers."

The current widespread query about identity comes not from a position of weakness and decline. More than ever before, the Anabaptist-related family of faith exists and is growing worldwide, in over sixty countries and hundreds of socio-cultural contexts. Many churches are actively engaged locally and nationally, trying to be authentic incarnations of the Gospel, exercising the particular gifts which come from an Anabaptist-related identity.

But what is "Anabaptist" identity? Meeting in Asia (January, 1997), the Mennonite World Conference (MWC) Faith and Life Council began a process for member churches to give and receive counsel about their lives as Anabaptist Christians. What indeed does it mean to believe and act as Anabaptist Christians today, not only in thousands of different local settings but also as a global family of faith? MWC members conversed with one another in response to this question when they met in South America (July, 2000) and in Africa (2003).

Of course, one condition for useful conversation on contemporary identity is a common historical point of reference. So MWC asked C. Arnold Snyder, internationally recognized historian of Anabaptism and experienced cross-cultural teacher, for help. Is it possible to speak of an "historical core" of Anabaptist-related identity? In spite of significant diversity from the beginning, can one identify a "common core" of conviction and practice in early Anabaptism? "I think so," Snyder responded, "and I will do my best to summarize it simply and clearly."

This booklet is the welcome result. The response to Snyder's teaching, when it first appeared in MWC's quarterly publications (*Courier*, *Correo*) in 1998, confirmed its importance, timeliness, and helpfulness on all continents.

This booklet should not be received as a normative or exhaustive statement for the faith and life of contemporary Anabaptist-related churches. But it can be taken as an indispensable text of reference for all who seek a succinct and reliable articulation of the common historical core of Anabaptist identity—one element in the process of letting Anabaptist Christianity be powerfully relevant even today, both locally and globally.

Larry Miller, Executive Secretary,
Mennonite World Conference
Strasbourg, France

Introduction

All farmers know that in order to grow healthy plants that bear fruit, three things are necessary: good seed, good soil, and careful cultivation. The choice of seed is crucial. Anyone who plants a mango seed and hopes to harvest oranges will be very disappointed. No amount of fertilizer will change the nature of the plant, contained as it was in the seed. But choosing and planting the right seed is not sufficient. The seed must be planted in fertile ground, or it withers and dies; and the young plants must be nourished and cared for, if one expects to harvest fruit.

Think of our churches as plants. Our church family first saw the light in the sixteenth century. It sprang from an Anabaptist seed. That original seed found fertile soil, was cultivated and nurtured, and produced an abundant harvest. The seeds of that harvest have been transplanted throughout the world now for almost 500 years. The basic nature of the seed is still visible in the plant, although cultivation and different climates have also changed the plant in important ways.

This booklet will describe the nature of the Anabaptist seed. Who were the Anabaptists? What beliefs did they hold in common? Like good farmers, the more we know about the nature of the seed we are planting, the more we will know more about the kind of soil, cultivation, and even pruning that may be necessary in order to produce abundant fruit in our place and time.

Who Were the Anabaptists?

The Anabaptists were people who were inspired by reforming ideas that were circulating in the 1520s in Europe, at the time of the Reformation. A few early Anabaptists were educated people, but Anabaptism was above all a reform of the common people. They were called "Anabaptists" or "re-baptizers" because they insisted that water baptism should be reserved for adults only. This conviction led them to baptize one another as adults, even though they had been baptized earlier, as infants.

The first adult baptism took place in Zurich, Switzerland, in January 1525. In spite of the fact that political authorities everywhere quickly declared the movement to be illegal, the baptizers continued to grow and flourish, practicing their faith in secret. In a few short years there were groups of baptizers throughout all of Europe, from The Netherlands to Poland to Slovakia. They called each other "brothers and sisters in Christ."

The Nature of this Study

Like all movements "from below," the baptizing movement included individuals who believed and practiced unique things. There was a lot of diversity among the baptizers. But at the same time, there was also a "core" of Anabaptist doctrine and practice that is visible in the court testimonies and writings that have survived. It is this "core" of doctrine and practice that we will describe.

Introduction

Our study of Anabaptist roots will be divided into three main sections.

1. **Anabaptist Doctrines**: What Christian teachings did the majority of Anabaptists think were central to their faith?
2. **Anabaptist Church Ordinances**: What church practices did the Anabaptists believe were essential to maintaining a faithful church?
3. **Anabaptist Discipleship**: What kind of a Christian life did Anabaptists expect from church members?

Although based on more comprehensive studies, the material in this booklet was composed in this form at the request of the Mennonite World Conference. It was intended to provide a basis for worldwide discussion about the essentials of Anabaptist-Mennonite faith and practice. The material was first published in 1998 as a three-part series in the English and Spanish versions of the Mennonite World Conference periodical, *Courier/Correo* and subsequently also in the *Canadian Mennonite* in 1999. The material appears here virtually unchanged.

In keeping with the original intent, which was to foster study, reflection, and discernment, we have added "questions for discussion" at the end of each major section.

For those who may wish to use this material as the basis for ongoing group study, there are twelve such sections, with corresponding questions.

Heart-felt thanks to Larry Miller and the staff of the Mennonite World Conference for supporting this publication, and for their work in encouraging international dialogue within the worldwide Christian and Mennonite fellowship.

1. Anabaptist Doctrines

Common Christian Teachings

Anabaptist doctrines were not brand new inventions, or even very distinctive in substance. Almost all the Anabaptists, when asked to give an account of their faith, simply repeated the Apostles' Creed, which they called the "Twelve Articles of the Faith," or simply "the Faith."

In their early catechisms, the Anabaptists taught the Apostles' Creed and the Lord's Prayer to their children and to converts. When they were asked what they believed, it was altogether common for Anabaptists to answer "I believe in God the Father, in Jesus Christ the only begotten Son of God, our Lord and Savior, and in the Holy Spirit."

> **We must rightly know the Father, Son, and Holy Spirit, that they are the true, living God ... This God has created us, has redeemed us, has taught and enlightened us ...; in him we must believe.**
> **(Dirk Philips, d. 1568)**

Anabaptism and the Reformation

The Anabaptists were part of the Reformation movement. They agreed with Luther, Zwingli, and Calvin that salvation is by faith, not by sacraments or works of penance. They also agreed with the reformers that the final authority for Christians is the Bible. Although the Anabaptists left the Roman Catholic church, as did other Protestants, the Anabaptists did not agree with the more famous reformers on all points.

What made the Anabaptists a distinctive church reform movement was the way they emphasized and interpreted common Christian and Reformation teachings, as we will see below. The Anabaptist emphases on the authority of Scripture and the Holy Spirit, salvation through conversion by the living Spirit of God, and a life of discipleship were among the most important distinctions.

How Can We Know God's Will?

Scripture

Martin Luther had preached church reform on the basis of "Scripture alone." The Anabaptists agreed that this was a good starting point, but they were suspicious about what the phrase might mean. It is all well and good to say that the church should be reformed according to "Scripture alone," but who is qualified to interpret what Scripture says? The Protestant reformers soon made it clear that the learned theologians were the ones who were "best fitted" to interpret Scripture.

Holy Spirit

The early Anabaptists agreed that Scripture should be the norm of reform, but they did not agree that the learned doctors were the ones best fitted to interpret the Scriptures.

They believed that the best interpreters of Scripture were those who had received the Holy Spirit. This meant, they said, that an illiterate peasant who has received the gift of the Holy Spirit is a better interpreter of God's Word than a learned theologian who lacks the Spirit.

God's commandment does not consist in the letter, but in the power which the Spirit gives.
(Hans Hut, d. 1527)

We can say that the Anabaptists taught "Scripture and Spirit, together" rather than "Scripture alone." This early Anabaptist idea was radical in the extreme, especially because it opened the interpretation of Scripture to all, educated and non-educated, men and women alike. The political authorities considered all of this politically dangerous and theologically irresponsible. But to the Anabaptists, discerning the will of God was something that all believers were expected to do.

He who does not have the Spirit and presumes to find it in Scripture, looks for light and finds darkness....
(Hans Denck, d. 1527)

Community

In fact, the Anabaptists themselves soon found it necessary to modify their teaching on "Scripture and Spirit." Some individual baptizers had begun prophesying and doing questionable things, claiming to be "led by the Spirit." How were "the spirits" to be tested?

One way to test the spirits was to discern both letter and spirit in the gathered congregation of believers. One very early Anabaptist document recommends that the brothers and sisters read Scripture together, and then "the one to whom God has given understanding shall explain it." This process of congregational discernment provided one way of placing some controls on the interpretation of Scripture and prophecy.

Christ

A second measure of spiritual claims emerged later, after some Anabaptists had been led to disaster by so-called prophets. Menno Simons especially emphasized that all spiritual claims must be measured by the life and the words of Christ. In this way, the "testing of the spirits" was returned to the discerning congregation, and to Jesus Christ and the scriptural witness about him.

By the Spirit, Word, actions, and example of Christ, all must be judged until the Last Judgment.
(Menno Simons, d. 1561)

How may Christians discern God's will? The Anabaptist answer took common Christian elements, but blended them in a new way. God's will is revealed in Scripture, interpreted by all believers through the power of the Holy Spirit, discerned in community, and tested by the measure of Christ.

FOR DISCUSSION

1. How is God's will discerned and communicated in your church community?
2. How is God's Spirit invited to speak in the process of discerning God's will?
3. How are the words of Scripture interpreted in your church community?
4. Read 1 Corinthians 3:11. In what ways is the person of Christ, his life, and his words, the measure of God's will for you and your church community?
5. Are there limits to discipleship? Read Matthew 5:43-48 and discuss the practical meaning of verse 48.

How Are We Saved?

Salvation by Faith

Luther, Zwingli, and Calvin said that human beings are saved by faith in Christ alone, without any works of penance. The Anabaptists also took "salvation by faith" very seriously, but explained the process of salvation differently.

For one thing, the Anabaptists believed that faith was something that only adults could understand. This had implications for baptism, which the Anabaptists believed should be reserved as an outer sign of a conscious inner faith.

In the second place, the Anabaptists believed that in order to arrive at faith, adults had to hear the Word, repent, and believe. But more than just "believing," the Anabaptists said that coming to faith meant being born again.

> **If we are to become free in the spirit and healthy in the soul ... then this must take place through a rebirth.**
> **(Balthasar Hubmaier, d. 1528)**

Being born again was an active spiritual process that had to include a conscious choice by individuals. And finally, the Anabaptists believed that a true faith would have to bear fruit in daily life.

So, although the Anabaptists agreed with the Protestant reformers that sinners are saved by faith in Christ, without any works of penance, they nevertheless understood the process of salvation in their own way. This led to a different kind of church reform and a different kind of church.

Grace, Predestination, and Free Will

Martin Luther believed that God's gift of grace was "irresistible." He thought that when God decided to give faith to a sinner, that sinner had no choice but to accept and believe. Such a person had been predestined to salvation.

The Anabaptists did not agree. They believed that God offered grace, but did not force it on anyone. Human beings had to exercise their free wills, said the Anabaptists, and could choose to either accept God's gift of faith, or refuse it.

One consequence of believing that God's grace was irresistible was that salvation was put beyond the reach of human beings. The Protestant reformers found great consolation in this: The gift of faith and salvation was a pure gift of God that no human being could change. But a further consequence was that in the predestinarian view, there was no real human responsibility in the matter of salvation. Salvation was pure grace that took place in the heavenly realms.

The Anabaptists agreed that salvation was a gift of grace, and could not be earned. But they read in many places in the New Testament that believers were to do their part as well. God's gift of faith, they believed, brought with it responsibility. Human beings needed to do their part in response to God's gift of faith.

Conversion and Regeneration

Martin Luther believed that the gift of faith changed one's standing before God, but did not necessarily change the sinner into a saint. In Protestant theology, being predestined to salvation might modify human behavior, but it would never change the basically sinful nature of human beings.

The Anabaptists did not agree. They believed that when God offered the gift of faith, this was an offer of spiritual power.

Those who accepted God's offer were not simply "justified" in heaven, they were reborn in the here and now. Faith enabled sinners to "put on Christ" and to receive the Spirit's power.

> **The regenerating Word must first be heard and believed with a sincere heart before regeneration, the putting on of Christ, and the impulsion of the Holy Ghost can follow.**
>
> **(Menno Simons, d. 1561)**

God's grace regenerates former sinners and makes them into new creatures. Believers who have been born again and regenerated by the Holy Spirit have been fitted to interpret and understand God's will in Scripture and to live new lives.

Faith and Works

So it was that although the Anabaptists said that believers are saved by faith, and not by works of penance, the Anabaptists thought that the reformers had not gone far enough when they said that human beings are saved by faith alone, without any works whatsoever.

They agreed that salvation comes only as a gift of God in Christ. But, they said, those who have received the gift of faith and have believed in Christ, become new creatures.

They necessarily do the works of love, because they have been regenerated by the power of the Holy Spirit. Having faith means having received power.

From an early catechism

Q: How many kinds of faith are there?
A: Two kinds, namely a dead one and a living one.

Q: What is a dead faith?
A: One that is unfruitful and without the works of love, James 2.

Q: What is a living faith?
A: One that produces the fruits of the Spirit and works through love, Galatians 5.

(Balthasar Hubmaier, d. 1528)

Discipleship

In Protestant theology, someone who had been predestined to receive the gift of faith was a sinner justified before God. For the Anabaptists, someone who had accepted God's gift of faith was a regenerated being who had "put on Christ" and started on the way of discipleship.

When the Anabaptists spoke about salvation, they never talked about being "justified by faith." For them salvation was a life process that called for perseverance to the end. Walking the Christian way required self-sacrifice, actively choosing the narrow way, and human effort. The phrase the Anabaptists used constantly was "the obedience of faith." Believing in the forgiveness of sins through Christ meant that one had gone through a process of repentance and conversion, and had set out to be a disciple, a follower of Christ in this life, in word and deed. And, the measure of the disciple and member of the Body of Christ was always Jesus Christ, the head.

FOR DISCUSSION

1. How does the Anabaptist understanding of salvation compare with your own and that of your church?

2. Does being "born again" mean that
   a. we have been accepted by God
   b. we have received power to become new creatures
   c. both of the above?

3. What are the strengths and/or limitations of understanding salvation as depending on the "obedience of faith"?

4. Read Romans 4:13; 23-25 and also James 2:14-17; 19-22 and discuss.

Consequences of Anabaptist Doctrines

Although it should be clear that the Anabaptists were not innovators in Christian doctrine, and in important ways were followers of the Protestant reformers, still the way that the Anabaptists interpreted common Christian teachings had very real consequences for the kind of a church they planted, and for the kind of a church we have inherited. We will explore these consequences in more detail in future studies. We can conclude with a few observations.

A Church of Believers, Born of the Spirit, Centered on Christ

One consequence of the way the Anabaptists discerned the will of God was that they assumed that all members were believers who had been born of the Spirit. There were to be no privileged "priestly" interpreters of God's will in this church, but rather a community made up of interpreting and discerning members. This community was brought into being as a result of the activity of the Holy Spirit. It was a community whose discernment was measured by the person and the words of Christ.

Biblical Literacy

The Anabaptist emphasis on a church of believers meant that all church members were urged to become biblically literate. Even though the majority of Anabaptists could neither read nor write, they nevertheless knew large portions of Scripture by memory, organized topically. Time and again Anabaptists in prison astounded their captors by reciting from memory the biblical foundations of their beliefs, chapter and verse.

Members were expected to own their own faith, and to be able to explain and defend it biblically. The court records demonstrate an astounding amount of biblical knowledge on the part of ordinary men and women who had become Anabaptists.

A Visible Church

A consequence of the Anabaptist understanding of salvation was that the true church would be a very visible church, made up of those who had openly chosen to say "yes" to God's offer of grace in Christ. The church would not simply be "known to God alone," but should be evident to any human observer. This church would be recognized by the repentance, rebirth, and new life of its members. It would be a church of obedient disciples, pledged to following after their Lord and Master, Jesus Christ.

FOR DISCUSSION

Anabaptist doctrines led to a vision of the church as a community of disciples, born again by the Spirit of God, discerning God's will together. This was a beautiful vision, but—

1. Is it a useful or practical vision for your church today?
2. What obstacles stand in the way of realizing this vision of church community?
3. In what ways does your church encourage biblical literacy for its members?
4. In what ways is your church a "visible" church of believers and disciples?

2. Anabaptist Church Ordinances

Anabaptist doctrines, as we have seen, were not particularly new or distinctive. Almost all Anabaptists held orthodox trinitarian beliefs, and they also agreed with the basic principles of the Protestant Reformation. But there were also significant differences. The Anabaptist church reform movement began when some believers instituted church practices that differed from Catholic and Protestant practices. The ordinance that sealed a separate reforming direction was adult baptism.

Description of the first adult baptisms in Zurich

After fear lay greatly upon them, they called upon God in heaven, that he should show mercy to them. Then George [Blaurock] arose and asked Conrad [Grebel] for God's sake to baptize him; and this he did. After that he baptized the others also.

Sacraments

Martin Luther posed a direct challenge to Roman Catholic church practices. The Roman Catholic church taught that there were seven Christian "sacraments." A sacrament was a visible sign that conferred divine grace. For example, in the sacrament of baptism, the visible sign was the water. When an ordained priest baptized an infant in water, there was said to be a corresponding internal action of grace that removed the stain of original sin from the soul of the infant.

Likewise in the Mass, after the visible elements of bread and wine had been blessed by the priest, the substance of the bread and wine became the actual body and blood of Christ (transubstantiation). According to Roman Catholic teaching, there was no salvation outside the church and its seven sacraments. And of course, only ordained clergy had the power to dispense the sacraments.

The Protestant reformers argued that salvation was by faith alone, and was not mediated by the sacraments or the priests of the church. Many people were ready to agree that grace was not mediated by sacraments, but in the 1520s it was not clear what the biblical view of sacraments should be and what should take the place of the older view.

The Anabaptists, like other evangelical church reformers, wanted to base their reforms entirely on the Word of God. On the basis of their study of Scripture, the Anabaptists came to believe that a church that was reformed according to the scriptural pattern would practice at least three basic church ordinances: *Baptism of Believers*, *Church Discipline*, and *The Lord's Supper.*

These church ordinances formed the core of early Anabaptist church practice. A fourth ordinance, foot-washing, was added later in the sixteenth century.

Baptism

Baptism of Believers

The baptism of believing adults was the most visible identifying mark of the Anabaptist movement. The essential scriptural argument for adult baptism was taken from the "Great Commission" of Jesus: Matthew 28:19-20. In those verses the Anabaptists read a clear biblical command concerning baptism: First go forth and teach (proclaim the Word), and then after teaching, baptize. Following baptism, new Christians are to be taught to live lives of obedience to Christ's commands.

Go therefore and make disciples of all nations, baptizing them in the name of the Father and of the Son and of the Holy Spirit, and teaching them to obey everything that I have commanded you.
MATTHEW 28:19-20

The scriptural order was clear to the Anabaptists, and none of it, they insisted, could possibly apply to newborn infants. Infants and small children cannot understand teaching about salvation, nor can they believe it, repent, and promise to live lives of obedience after their baptisms. For the Anabaptists the scriptural meaning of baptism was clear: Baptism was not a sacrament to be used by priests, it was a external sign of interior faith.

The early Anabaptists very often spoke of a "threefold baptism," by which they meant that one was first baptized by the Holy Spirit, then in water, and finally, in blood.

Baptism of the Spirit

The Anabaptists rejected the idea that water could become a sacrament that conveyed grace. They maintained that "the water is just water."

Strictly speaking, then, the water of baptism itself was not holy. It was the *inner baptism of the Spirit* that was primary and essential.

It was this spiritual baptism that led believers to repentance, faith, and commitment. It was this baptism of the Spirit that regenerated believers, and granted them the spiritual power to become obedient disciples.

Baptism in the Spirit and fire is to make alive and whole again the confessing sinner with the fire of the divine Word by the Spirit of God.
(Balthasar Hubmaier, d. 1528)

Baptism in Water

Water baptism was secondary. It was an outward "confession" or a "testimony" to what had happened inwardly. Nevertheless, just because water baptism was a second step, this did not mean that water baptism was optional or unimportant to the Anabaptists. Baptism in water had a crucial role to play in establishing the visible Body of Christ on earth. Water baptism was a necessary outer witness to the inner spiritual change.

When believers accepted water baptism, this was their public seal, promise, and *commitment to the church*. Besides being a response of obedience to a scriptural command, the water was understood to be a "covenant of a good conscience" before God and the congregation (1 Peter 3:21). Water baptism could not to be ignored or lightly set aside.

Baptism in water in the name of the Father, and the Son, and the Holy Spirit ... is nothing other than a public confession and testimony of internal faith and commitment.

(Balthasar Hubmaier, d. 1528)

Baptism of Blood

The phrase "baptism of blood" rightly brings to mind martyrdom, which was a terrible reality for more than 4,000 Anabaptists in the sixteenth century. But the phrase had a less fatal meaning as well.

The Anabaptists believed that after the baptisms of Spirit and water, they would still face a constant

The flesh must daily be killed since it wants only to live and reign according to its own lusts. Here the Spirit of Christ prevails and gains the victory. Then the person brings forth good fruits which give testimony of a good tree. Day and night he practices all those things which concern the praise of God and brotherly love. By this the old Adam is martyred, killed, and carried to the grave.

(Balthasar Hubmaier, d. 1528)

struggle against "the flesh" and "the world." There were human failings that had to be resisted constantly, and the power of the Spirit had to be invoked with the same constancy. This "killing of the old Adam" was a third, painful, and continuing "baptism." There was an ascetic, otherworldly tone to Anabaptist spirituality that is captured by the phrase "baptism of blood." The Anabaptists expected the life of faith to be a continual, but successful, struggle against temptation.

But in the sixteenth century, the "baptism of blood" often meant much more than just mortification of the flesh. It could mean a call to accept the fact that one's own blood would be shed. If believers were called to witness to the truth by accepting death, they had already prepared because of practice in the third baptism, the "burying of the old Adam," that was supposed to occur daily.

FOR DISCUSSION

1. How is baptism practiced in your church community?
2. Compare and contrast your understanding of the different dimensions of baptism, with the Anabaptist understanding of the "three-fold baptism."
3. Read Romans 6:1-4 and discuss its practical meaning for you and your church community.

Church Discipline

The Three-Fold Admonition

The public ordinance of baptism was important because it was a sign to the congregation that new believers bound themselves to church discipline. The scriptural basis for church discipline was found in Matthew 18:15-18. Those verses, said the Anabaptists, provided the proper, biblical order to be followed for the maintenance of a true church.

Confession and Absolution

One of the functions of church discipline, which the Anabaptists called "the ban," was to take the place of the old sacrament of penance (confession and absolution). The aim was to provide a way of confessing sin, forgiving it, and re-admitting the sinner back into the congregation.

In practice, however, a loving exercise of the ban proved to be difficult. Although "fraternal admonition"

If another member of the church sins against you, go and point out the fault when the two of you are alone. If the member listens to you, you have regained that one. But if you are not listened to, take one or two others along with you so that every word may be confirmed by the evidence of two or three witnesses. If the member refuses to listen to them, tell it to the church; and if the offender refuses to listen even to the church, let such a one be to you as a Gentile and a tax collector.

Matthew 18:15-18

was biblical in its foundation, and could be described as an ideal way of re-admitting the fallen into the congregation, in actual practice the ban soon became more an instrument of division than an instrument of forgiveness and union.

The Pure Church

A second function of the ban was to maintain a vital and reformed church. The Anabaptists were convinced the true church would be made up of those who had been regenerated by the Holy Spirit, and had become spiritual sons and daughters of God. Such "members of the Body of Christ" would live visibly new lives. Just as Christ was pure and holy, so also his members were to be pure and holy. The ban provided a way to maintain holiness and purity in the church.

Of course, this was a high calling that was not always attained. Nevertheless, the Anabaptists soon gained a reputation for being sober, upright, and honest people. There were actually several cases of people arrested on suspicion of being Anabaptist, simply because they had stopped cursing, gambling, and getting drunk. They were not released from jail until they had proven that their turn for the better had nothing to do with adult baptism.

Christians are members of Christ, and their body the temple of the Holy Spirit ... Jesus Christ has no unclean members, and the temple of the Holy Spirit is holy.
(Dirk Philips, d. 1568)

FOR DISCUSSION

1. In what ways is "fraternal admonition" practiced in your church community?
2. Read and compare 1 Corinthians 5:9-13 and 1 Corinthians 13:1-7.
3. Read Galatians 6:1-2. How can the church balance the call for purity, with the call for love and patience?

The Lord's Supper

A Memorial

All Anabaptists rejected the idea that there was a real, bodily presence of Christ in the elements of bread and wine. The bread, they said, was just bread, and the wine was just wine. The Lord's Supper was a memorial to be celebrated by baptized and disciplined believers, not a re-creation of Christ's sacrifice to be done by priests on behalf of sinners.

The Lord's Supper is a sign of the obligation to brotherly love just as water baptism is a symbol of the vow of faith. The water concerns God, the Supper our neighbor.

(Balthasar Hubmaier, d. 1528)

The key words of Scripture supporting this memorialist understanding of the Supper are found in 1 Corinthians 11:23-26. For the Anabaptists, Jesus' words "Do this in remembrance of me" indicated what the celebration of the Supper was supposed to signify: It was a remembering of Jesus' death and sacrifice and a "showing forth" of his death until his return.

The Lord Jesus on the night when he was betrayed took a loaf of bread, and when he had given thanks, he broke it and said: "This is my body that is for you. Do this in remembrance of me.

1 Corinthians 11:23-24

Celebrated Worthily

Believers' baptism and submission to church discipline were prerequisites for partaking in the Lord's Supper. Since the Lord's Supper was a celebration of unity in the Body of Christ, each member was to do a careful self-examination, to ensure that the Supper was being celebrated "worthily." In this way the ban prepared the way for the Lord's Supper, since unworthy members were disciplined and called to repentance before celebrating together. Fraternal admonition was part of "discerning the body." The Supper, the Anabaptists said, was meant to be celebrated by those who had a living faith, and who demonstrated their faith in their daily living.

The bread and wine are nothing but memorial symbols of Christ's suffering and death....

(Balthasar Hubmaier, d. 1528)

Examine yourselves, and only then eat of the bread and drink of the cup. For all who eat and drink without discerning the body, eat and drink judgement against themselves.

1 Corinthians 11:28-29

Recommitment to Brothers and Sisters

In Anabaptist congregations in the sixteenth century, celebrating the Lord's Supper was a powerful sign of renewed commitment to the fellowship. By sharing the loaf and the cup of the Lord, members were signifying their willingness to give their lives for one another.

In the sixteenth century this was not taken lightly. Anabaptist prisoners were almost always tortured, and asked to give the names of their fellow church members. In this context of persecution, celebrating the Lord's Supper together was a powerful symbol of common commitment and purpose.

[The Supper is] a public sign... of the love in which one brother obligates himself to another before the congregation that just as they now break and eat bread with each other and share and drink the cup, likewise they wish now to sacrifice and shed their body and blood for one another....

(Balthasar Hubmaier, d. 1528)

FOR DISCUSSION

Think of how the Lord's Supper is practiced in your church community.

1. What are the symbolic meanings given to the Lord's Supper?

2. Does the Lord's Supper also have a practical dimension of reconciliation and/or mutual aid in your church practice?
3. Read 1 Corinthians 11:23-24. Compare and contrast your church practice of the Supper with the Anabaptist practice.

Footwashing

The ordinance of footwashing was not practiced in all the early Anabaptist congregations. The South German Anabaptist leader Pilgram Marpeck (D. 1556) spoke of footwashing as a church ordinance, but the practice became most widespread in The Netherlands, where it entered the confessions that were produced in the late sixteenth and seventeenth centuries.

Then he poured water into a basin and began to wash the disciples' feet and to wipe them with the towel that was tied around him.
JOHN 13:5

The practice of footwashing was considered to be an "ordinance" primarily because Jesus "instituted

We also confess a washing of the feet of the saints ... as a sign of true humiliation; but yet more particularly as a sign to remind us of the true washing—the washing and purification of the soul in the blood of Christ.
(DORDRECHT CONFESSION ARTICLE XI, 1632)

and commanded" the practice. Its symbolic meaning relating to humility and continued purification was explained best by Dirk Philips, bishop and co-worker in The Netherlands with Menno Simons. Late in the seventeenth century, the adoption of the Dordrecht Confession by Swiss Brethren included also the adoption of footwashing as an ordinance, and the practice became accepted in the South as well.

FOR DISCUSSION

1. Is footwashing practiced in your church community?
2. Read John 13:4-17 and I Timothy 5:10.
3. Is Jesus' action an appropriate public symbol for disciples to also perform?

Consequences of Anabaptist Ordinances

Church ordinances can be thought of as doctrines made visible in ritual practice. Anabaptist church ordinances can be thought of as providing a sketch or outline of Anabaptist doctrinal emphases.

A Church of Born-Again Believers

The ordinance of baptism lay close to the heart of Anabaptist belief, and it gave shape to a particular kind of church. It was a church that would be made up of persons who had answered God's call in a conscious and visible way. Believers' baptism was meant to insure that the "Body of Christ" would be composed of reborn members; the ban was to keep the Body united in belief and action; the Supper and Footwashing were to strengthen commitment between the brothers and sisters of the church.

A Visible Church

A church composed of people who agreed to the Anabaptist understanding of baptism would not be a church of a whole territory, or an "invisible" church, known to God alone. This church would be visibly composed of those who were prepared to make a public commitment to follow Jesus on the way to the cross. It was a church whose visible holiness was to be maintained by an attentive discipline and strengthened by the Lord's Supper and Footwashing.

A Church Relying on the Holy Spirit

The Anabaptist church ordinances make it clear how much the Anabaptists emphasized the spiritual dimension of the Christian life. The authority for adult baptism in water was granted by the scriptural command of the Lord, but the actual inward baptism was granted by the living Spirit of God.

Likewise, the power to become disciples and to persevere on the narrow way was a power granted by the Holy Spirit. It was the Holy Spirit that made it possible for believers to resist temptation and to live new lives. It was the same Holy Spirit that enabled thousands of Anabaptists to persevere even unto death.

It is important to note also that the baptisms of Spirit, water, and blood fell to individual women and men alike, and called for their free-willed obedience to the commands of the Lord and faithfulness to the community. When disciples were being called, the Holy Spirit did not recognize gender. Anabaptist churches were noted for the high participation of women and men from every rank of society. Approximately a third of all Anabaptist martyrs were women.

FOR DISCUSSION

The church's beliefs are made visible in the communal practices and the individual lives of its members.

1. In what ways do the ordinances practiced in your church community make visible your faith?
2. In what ways is the power of the Holy Spirit manifested in and through the ordinances of your church community?

3.

Discipleship: Living the Faith

A Spirituality of Integrity

The Anabaptists were sure that there had to be a necessary connection between an inner, spiritual baptism and an outward baptism in water, between an inner faith in God and an outer walk of obedience, following in Christ's footsteps. The Anabaptists were convinced that the Christian life must be one of integrity, in which a living, spiritual reality expresses itself in a corresponding outward behavior. The Spirit of Christ will produce a Christ-like life.

Because Christ is the root and the vine and we are grafted into him through faith, even as the sap rises from the root and makes the branches fruitful, even so the Spirit of Christ rises from the root, Christ, into the branches and twigs to make them root, and bear only corresponding fruit.

(Peter Riedemann, d. 1556)

In what concrete ways would spiritual rebirth be visible outwardly, in one's daily life? The answers to this question were not entirely obvious in the beginning. But as the Anabaptist movement progressed, more visible signs of discipleship were clarified. The Anabaptists became increasingly sure that among the visible fruits of the Spirit of Christ they would find: *Truth-Telling, Economic Sharing,* and *Pacifism.*

If any want to become my followers, let them deny themselves and take up their cross and follow me.
Mark 8:34

Truth-Telling

Civil Oaths

Being a disciple meant obeying the commands of the Lord. For sixteenth century believers one of the most difficult sayings of Jesus was his command to "swear not at all."

Political society in the sixteenth century was bound together by oaths of loyalty. Oaths were required on joining a guild, on renewing citizenship in a city, and in all courts of law. To refuse to swear oaths in the sixteenth century would mean placing oneself outside of the political and social order. Perhaps for this reason, consensus on oath-refusal emerged only over time.

But I say to you, Do not swear at all ... Let your word be "Yes, Yes" or "No, No"; anything more than this comes from the evil one.
Matthew 5:34; 37

Integrity

In the end, the Anabaptists agreed that Jesus' word was final: Christians should be truth-tellers, whose yes means yes, and whose no means no, regardless of the civil consequences. This caused them no end of legal trouble.

The "refusal to swear oaths" was more than just obedience to a literal "command." It was also in complete harmony with the Anabaptist insistence on spiritual integrity.

Born-again disciples of Jesus Christ should be expected not only to tell the truth, but to live the truth. Members of the Body of Christ on earth should be people whose words and deeds correspond absolutely. The sin of untruthfulness was one for which Anabaptist members would be admonished and disciplined.

All who are planted into the body of the church through faith in Christ, will not swear as the children of the world do. Rather they confess and live the truth without any additions, with a pure heart.

(Testimony of Hans Marquart, 1532)

FOR DISCUSSION

1. Does your church community provide instruction concerning the non-swearing of oaths?
2. In what ways is the living of a life of integrity and truthfulness a part of your church experience?
3. In what ways is spiritual rebirth made visible in the life of your church community?

Economic Sharing

Sharing Earthly Goods

One of the testimonies of faith and regeneration expected of all Anabaptist believers was economic sharing with those who had need. Such "yielding" of one's possessions was a visible sign that one had died to self and risen in Christ, and had totally committed oneself to the Body of Christ on earth. Spiritual "yielding" (*Gelassenheit*) should be made visible in a "yielding" of possession of material things.

Various passages of Scripture were commonly cited, but 1 John 3:16-18 was a favorite. As far as the early Anabaptists were concerned, a visible mark of unbelief was to "shut up one's bowels of compassion" against those in need. Matthew 25:31-46 (the sheep and the goats at the Last Judgment) was another favorite Scripture passage that spoke to this question.

In several Anabaptist communities in Moravia in the 1520s and 1530s and later with the Hutterites, economic sharing took the form of community of goods, where members gave up all claims to property. But even in

We know love by this, that he laid down his life for us—and we ought to lay down our lives for one another. How does God's love abide in anyone who has the world's goods and sees a brother or sister in need and yet refuses help? Little children, let us love, not in word or speech, but in truth and action.

1 John 3:16-18

the more numerous non-communal Anabaptist groups there was a "common purse" kept to help the needy.

Being a member meant caring for the poor, the widows, and the orphans, and generally living as "members of one body." There were also some notable instances of generosity outside the community of faith. The Anabaptists believed that those who had been born again would live their economic lives in a way that showed forth their love of God above all and the love of their neighbors as themselves.

Whoever has a true faith will share with a needy member and not keep anything as personal property.

(Testimony of Barbli with the wooden leg, Bern, Switzerland, May 1529)

FOR DISCUSSION

1. In what ways does your church community teach and encourage economic sharing among members and outside the church?
2. Should economic matters be the church's business?
3. Do you believe that "true faith" is tested by the measure of generosity?

Pacifism

The followers of Jesus must live in the world, but how should they relate to the evil that is in the world? The Anabaptists had to go through a painful process of learning and discernment until they arrived at consensus on this question.

Pacifist Roots

From the start there had been Anabaptists who were sure that following in Jesus' footsteps provided clear guidance: Disciples suffer with Christ; they do not inflict suffering on others through violence.

The Gospel and its adherents are not to be protected by the sword, nor are they thus to protect themselves.
(Conrad Grebel, d. 1526)

Among the very first Anabaptists, and in all groups thereafter, there were brothers and sisters who were convinced that "taking the sword" was never allowed to Christians.

Apocalyptic Challenge

But from the start there were also Anabaptists who were sure that they were living in the End Times, and that Jesus would return in a matter of months or years.

Among these Anabaptists were people who prophesied in the name of God that the time for turning the other cheek had passed. The End Times had arrived, and with them a new dispensation, a new revelation, and a new task for God's chosen people. "The elect" should take the sword "in these last days," to prepare for the coming of the New Jerusalem.

These prophecies proved to be tragically false, but not before many Anabaptists had died by the sword, thinking that they were doing God's will in preparing the way for the return of Jesus. The most spectacular and terrible occurrence happened in the "Anabaptist city" of Münster in northern Germany, which was taken by armed Anabaptists and defended for almost a year and a half (1534-1535).

The Lord wishes ... that we and all true Christians in this time not only be allowed to turn away the power of the ungodly with the sword, but even more, that the sword be put into the hands of his people to avenge all that is unjust and evil in the whole world ... The time is at hand.
(Bernhard Rothmann, writing from Anabaptist Münster in 1535)

Painful Lesson

Münster was a horror and a tragedy, but it finally settled the question of violence for the Anabaptists. After Münster the Anabaptists came to agreement that in questions of discipleship, the words and the example of Jesus were final, and could not be set aside until Jesus himself set them aside. The infallible guideline for discerning God's will is Jesus Christ.

Even though Elijah himself were to come, he would not have anything to teach contrary to the foundations and doctrine of Christ and the apostles.
(Menno Simons, d. 1561)

Once this Christocentric principle of discernment was

accepted, it was clear to the Anabaptists that disciples of Jesus Christ must put away the sword, unconditionally.

- There was, first of all, the example of Christ himself, who prayed "not my will, but yours be done," and who allowed himself to be crucified. Disciples of Jesus, if faced with a similar choice of resisting Caesar, will do as Christ did, not resist, and accept death instead.
- In the second place, there was a clear scriptural command of the Lord that forbade violence and even hatred of enemies, and instead commanded love.
- And finally, participating in violence contradicted the principle of spiritual integrity, that believers who live by the Spirit of Christ will show forth the love of God in their daily lives. Christians wield spiritual weapons, not weapons of iron and steel.

By 1540 the Anabaptists had achieved wide consensus, that reborn, baptized Christians will refuse to participate in violence. But there remained some questions to be settled which have persisted to this day: How should pacifist Christians relate to the world of evil and violence?

They who are baptized inwardly with Spirit and fire, and externally with water, according to the Word of the Lord, have no weapons except patience, hope, silence, and God's Word.

(Menno Simons, d. 1561)

Nonresistance

The majority of Anabaptists came to be guided by the words of Jesus in Matthew 5:39: Do not resist an evildoer. They understood these words to mean: Separate from the world, and don't become involved in its governance.

These "nonresistant" Anabaptists were not anarchists; they were separatists, which is quite a different thing. They believed that God had ordained governments to keep order in the world (Romans 13), but they believed that Christians would live according to the "perfection of Christ," and leave governance to non-Christians. Governments were not Christian, but they were necessary and were to be obeyed, insofar as they did not command things contrary to God's Word.

> **You have heard that it was said, "An eye for an eye and a tooth for a tooth." But I say to you, Do not resist an evildoer.**
> MATTHEW 5:38-39

For nonresistant Anabaptists it seemed clear that the followers of Jesus would have to separate from the world and leave it behind. Christians were called to establish outposts of the Kingdom of Heaven, here on earth. They would live as disciples and followers of Jesus in these communities, but they could expect only suffering in the world, on this side of eternity.

> **Governmental authority has its place outside Christ, but not in Christ.**
> (PETER RIEDEMANN, D. 1556)

Nonviolence

Among the pacifist Anabaptists a small minority thought that the separation of the church from the world would not be so absolute. Pilgram Marpeck was committed to nonviolence, but he thought of the church more as an outpost of God's love whose mission was to actively radiate that love out into the world. It was a subtle but important shift in emphasis.

Do not be overcome by evil, but overcome evil with good.
Romans 12:21

In Marpeck's understanding, the followers of Jesus would not isolate themselves from the world as if trying to defend a citadel of purity. Rather, they would open the windows and the doors, show forth God's love to the world, and invite unbelievers to come in.

Marpeck's more active vision for the church was, however, in the minority in the sixteenth century. Most Anabaptists—in large part because of the fierce persecution they had to endure—became convinced that the church should be as separate from the world as humanly possible. The result was a separatist, inward-looking, and very quiet church tradition that sought to avoid trouble.

Christ forbade such violence and resistance, and commanded the children who possessed the Spirit of the New Testament to love, to bless their enemies, persecutors, and opponents, and to overcome them with patience.

(Pilgram Marpeck, d. 1556)

Discipleship

In the end, the difficult issue of violence was settled according to the principle of discipleship, with a view to the example of Jesus. Reborn disciples will follow Jesus. They will speak the truth and live the truth. They have renounced claims to earthly possessions. They will not return evil for evil, but will respond to evil with good.

In all these ways, the Anabaptists set out to live lives of spiritual integrity, in which their daily actions showed forth the living Spirit of God.

FOR DISCUSSION

1. How are the principles of peace taught and modeled in your church community?

2. How have members of your church, or your church as a whole, responded when they are victims of violence?

3. Is your church community withdrawn from conflict that takes place in the wider world, or does it take an active role in peacemaking outside the church?

4. In your experience, is teaching about peace in your church community primarily
   a. based on obedience to biblical command,
   b. rooted in spiritual rebirth and the spiritual disciplines?

5. In what ways might a disciple apply peace teaching to conflicts in the home?

4. Conclusion

We have presented a brief overview of the "core" of Anabaptist teaching, church ordinances, and the practices of daily living. Although the Anabaptist way was orthodox, and generally followed the Protestant path, it was undeniably a distinctive interpretation of the Christian way.

There is much that we can and should learn from the testimony of these faithful witnesses. Nevertheless, one seed alone cannot be expected to fill God's entire vineyard. One variety of grape cannot provide every kind of wine, from sweet to dry, red to white.

I would like to conclude by considering the Anabaptist seed and fruit in the larger context of God's vineyard. I would suggest that we take a wide view, rather than a narrow view, of God's work in the world.

A Rich Harvest from All Corners of God's Vineyard

In the sixteenth century it was commonly believed that there was only one truth, and that it could be embodied in only one Christian tradition. We are learning in our century to appreciate the different gifts and legacies preserved and brought to the common Christian table by all Christian traditions. Anabaptist-related believers have important things to offer to this common discussion, but something to learn as well.

Theological Reflection (Doctrines)

Thinking about the truths of the Christian faith and organizing and explaining those truths has enriched the Christian tradition from the beginning, and continues to enrich us. The Anabaptists did not feel called to the task of creative thinking in matters of doctrine. They were pleased simply to repeat the commonly accepted creeds. Not surprisingly, the "non-theological" nature of the Anabaptist seed has meant fruit and wine with a distinctly "non-theological" flavor.

We can be thankful that the continuing task of theological reflection has been cultivated in other parts of God's vineyard. There is much that Anabaptist-related churches can learn from theological conversation and reflection with other Christian traditions about the truths of our common faith.

Ritual and Symbolic Language (Church Ordinances)

The Anabaptists were concerned to establish church ordinances only on the basis of what Scripture had commanded explicitly. In the sixteenth century this meant radically simplifying the ritual and symbolic language that had evolved in the church for 1500 years. In its place, the Anabaptist tradition evolved a spare and simple "worship order" based on baptism, the ban, the Lord's Supper, and footwashing.

In other parts of God's vineyard, the liturgical Christian traditions have preserved the insight that the language of the Spirit is enriched by a grammar and a vocabulary that transcends, goes beyond, the mundane. In the beauty of ritual and symbolic action, these traditions convey the deep truth that as Christian believers and human beings, we can and must point beyond ourselves to the higher power and reality of God.

Anabaptist-related churches can learn much that is good from the traditions that have preserved this dimension of the Christian experience, namely, an appreciation of the spiritual power of ritual, symbol, aesthetic beauty, and architectural space.

Practical Spirituality (Discipleship)

The Anabaptist seed may not have produced a wine one would wish to label "theology" or "liturgy." But it did lead to a strong and distinctive vintage that we could call "practical spirituality." The Anabaptist tradition has thought and struggled much with issues of faithful living. It is this wine in particular that the Anabaptist tradition brings as its own offering to the common Christian table.

A practical Christian spirituality, as understood by the Anabaptists, would involve a delicate balance between the inner life of the spirit and the outer life that is lived in the world.

- A Christian becomes one by a baptism of the Spirit, which is followed by a baptism in water and a life of obedience.
- A life of discipleship will have to balance the spirit and the letter in discerning God's will.
- Discipleship must balance God's gift of grace, with human effort.

- Discipleship must balance dependence on God's regenerating Spirit with a disciple's free-willed obedience.
- Discipleship must balance personal, inner conviction against commitment and obedience to the community.

The consequences of "losing balance" in one direction or the other were evident already to the Anabaptists in the sixteenth century. Over-emphasizing spirit, grace, and the inner life could result in a denial of active discipleship in the world; over-emphasizing literal word, obedience, community, and the outer life could result in a legalism that lacked the living Spirit.

Maintaining Balance

There has been only one human being who achieved perfect balance, and he was the Son of God. As followers of Jesus we can and should look to the worldwide community of faith for insight, even in this matter of practical spirituality where our tradition has concentrated its energies.

The *Pentecostal and Charismatic traditions* bring forward the fundamental truth that being a Christian is much more than simply affirming the intellectual truth of historical events. Being a Christian means coming into, and growing into, a spiritual relationship with the living and creating power of God.

A continuing temptation in some parts of the Anabaptist tradition has been to emphasize obedience and discipleship within community. Sometimes it has been tempting to consider obedience an end in itself, as if salvation hinged on obeying particular rules. We can learn from Pentecostal and Charismatic Christians that obedience to church rules and orders is no substitute for nurturing and cultivating a vital life of the spirit.

The *Protestant traditions* have continued to insist that salvation flows from the mercy seat of God, and not in payment for human achievement. The Anabaptists wished to establish a careful balance between salvation as a gift of God, and a life of obedience as a response to God's grace.

In some cases the Anabaptist pendulum swung far to the side of "works," and over-valued the works of discipleship. At those times, Martin Luther's insight has provided a helpful corrective. Discipleship and obedience are, in the final analysis, also gifts of grace.

The *Anabaptist traditions* have refused to allow salvation and the spiritual life to be separated from a life of obedience and discipleship. The two belong together. Here is the particular seed, fruit, and vintage we have inherited from the Lord and our parents in the faith.

Nevertheless, in some parts of the Anabaptist tradition there has been a temptation to spiritualize the life of faith to the point that obedience and discipleship become optional, secondary, and not really central. At these times and places, it worthwhile to reflect again on the Anabaptist insight that the life of the spirit will be an incarnated life of discipleship, in which the love of Christ will be visibly evident.

FOR DISCUSSION

1. Does the image of maintaining balance between grace and obedience ring true for you? If so, in what ways might you and your church community work to achieve that balance?

2. Do you agree that thinking carefully about the doctrines of our faith is an important activity? In what ways does theological reflection happen in your church community?

3. Do you believe that symbolic and liturgical action has the capacity to communicate truths about the Christian faith? If so, what are some ways that the symbolic language of faith can be encouraged and nurtured in your church community?

4. In what ways does your church community encourage and nurture the spiritual life?

5. In what ways does your church community foster a life of active discipleship in the world?

6. And finally: What does it mean, in our place and time, to be a church that has grown from Anabaptist "seed?"

The answer to this question must come from our congregations around the world, from all parts of God's vineyard, as together we discern God's will at the start of a new millennium.

May God's grace flow freely and bear abundant fruit!

About the Author

C. Arnold Snyder is a professor of history at Conrad Grebel University College in Waterloo, Ontario. He is General Editor (with John Lapp) of the Global Mennonite History series published under the auspices of Mennonite World Conference, and former Managing Editor of Pandora Press (1995-2007). His most recent publication is *Following in the Footsteps of Christ: The Anabaptist Tradition* (2004), the nineteenth volume in the Traditions of Christian Spirituality series published by Orbis Books.

METHOD OF PAYMENT

❐ Check or Money Order
(payable to ***Good Books*** *in U.S. funds)*

❐ Please charge my:

❐ MasterCard ❐ Visa
❐ Discover ❐ American Express

\# ______________________________
exp. date ______________________________
Signature ______________________________

Name ______________________________
Address ______________________________
City ______________________________
State ______________________________
Zip ______________________________
Phone ______________________________
Email ______________________________

SHIP TO: (if different)
Name ______________________________
Address ______________________________
City ______________________________
State ______________________________
Zip ______________________________

Mail order to: **Good Books**
P.O. Box 419 • Intercourse, PA 17534-0419
Call toll-free: 800/762-7171
Fax toll-free: 888/768-3433
Prices subject to change.

Group Discounts for

From Anabaptist Seed

ORDER FORM

(U.S. Addresses Only)

If you would like to order multiple copies of ***From Anabaptist Seed*** by C. Arnold Snyder for groups you know or are a part of, use this form. (Discounts apply only for more than one copy.) Photocopy this page as often as you like.

The following discounts apply:

1 copy	$8.95
2-5 copies	$8.05 each (a 10% discount)
6-10 copies	$7.60 each (a 15% discount)
11-20 copies	$7.16 each (a 20% discount)
21-99 copies	$6.26 each (a 30% discount)
100 or more	$5.37 each (a 40% discount)

Prices subject to change.

Quantity		***Price***	***Total***
_____	copies of ***From Anabaptist Seed*** @	_______	_______
	PA residents add 6% sales tax		_______
	Shipping & Handling *(add 10%; $3.00 minimum)*		_______
	TOTAL		_______